After The Masquerade…

By. Willman E. Compton Jr.III

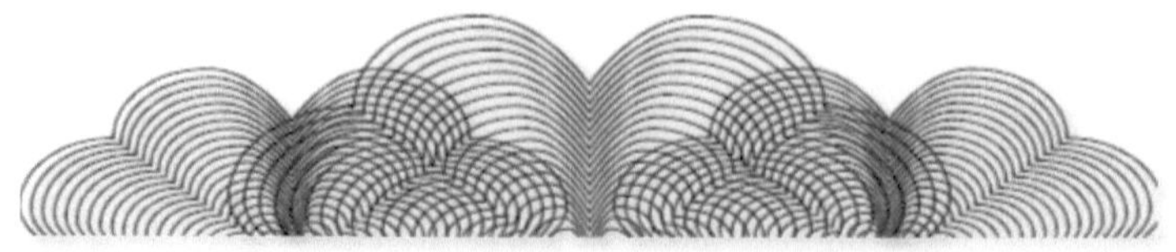

After The *Masquerade…*

We must deal with the Mess we made.

Rain Maker's Publishing Inc.

San Antonio, TX.

Printed by: http://www.lulu.com

International Standard Book Number:

978-0-557-43265-3

Cover Design & Book Layout: Willman Compton Jr

To Contact Author: WILLMANCOMPTON@ATT.NET

http://stores.lulu.com/willmancompton

Table of Contents

Table of Contents Continued

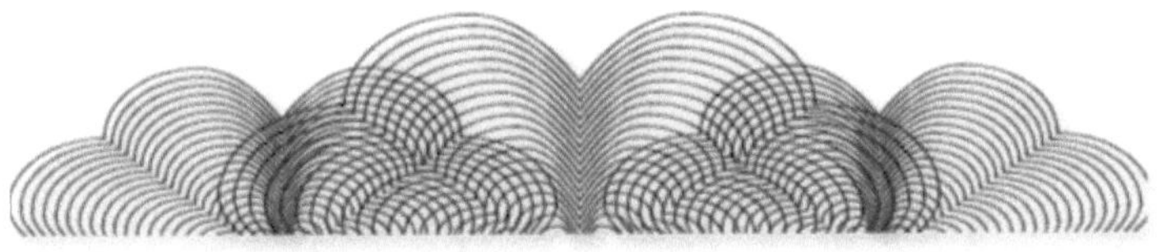

"If I had the opportunity
To put to words and tell my story
About some of the sweetest moments
Of my life along with some of the biggest mistakes
And hardest lessons I have learned
During the early years of
My walk with
Jesus Christ,
They would sound something like this...."

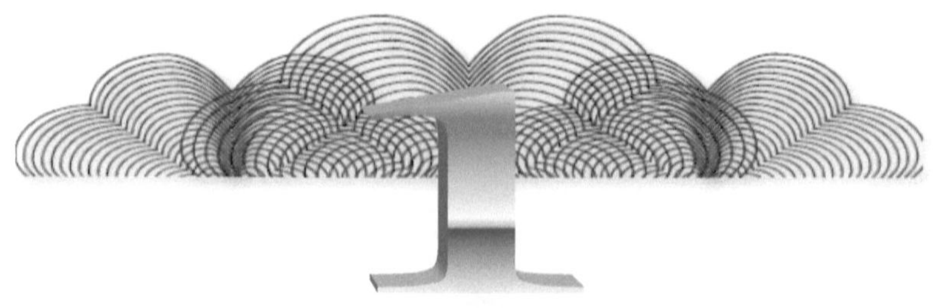

CHAPTER

During The Masquerade

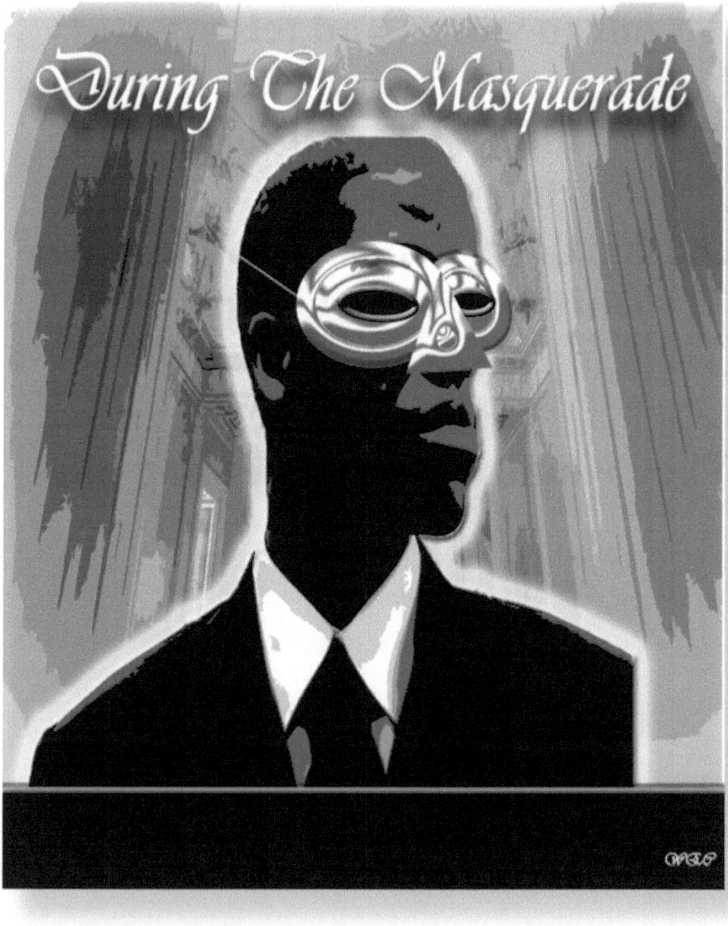

A MASQUERADE

(\ *mas - que - rade*\)

1: A social gathering of persons wearing

Bizarre masks and often fantastic costumes:

2: An action or an appearance that

Is merely just for show.

3: to assume the appearance

Of something one is not.

My son, pay
Attention to my wisdom;
Lend your ear to my understanding,
That you may preserve discretion,
And your lips may keep knowledge.
For the lips of an immoral woman
Drip honey, and her mouth is smoother
Than oil; but in the end she is bitter as
Wormwood, Sharp as a two-edged sword.
Her feet go down to death,
Her steps lay hold of hell.
Lest you ponder her path of life —her
Ways are unstable; you do not
Know them.

Proverbs 5:1-6 (NKJV)

A Text

It started with a text on my phone; now you're sitting next to me.

I can't believe you're in my home, but I don't want you to leave.

I can feel my pulse racing now and the room is getting hot like flames burning the floor.

I remember the feeling of your hands in mine and the thought of wanting more. But you got a man at home and it's breaking my heart.

I know playing with sin we can't win, and as temptations come I must flea. But she holds me close, and then spoke these words "she's only thinking of me."

So I just close my eyes and think to myself, my God I know this isn't right, but I feel so alone, please let me squeeze this woman tight and pretend she 's my own. As midday turns to dusk, and dusk fades into twilight; the only way I can see her face is from the moon and candlelight. I still think of the time when I kissed bitter tears in her eyes as they rolled down her sweet face, while knowing deep in my soul she couldn't stay, because he's waiting at her place. There are days I caught myself staring at the spot where we

Prayed, that the Lord's will would be done; and if it were his will that we would become as one.

As she walked out of my door she walked out of my life, she drove off in her car and never kissed me goodnight. As I slept I tossed and turned in my bed, warring with my desires all night. And only the Lord knows I was losing that fight. 24hrs had passed before you even called to say you're all right. So I stayed up pacing the floor because I went out on a limb. Then two days later, I got a text on my phone that said we couldn't talk anymore because now she's married to him.

Sorry,

End of text.

Empty

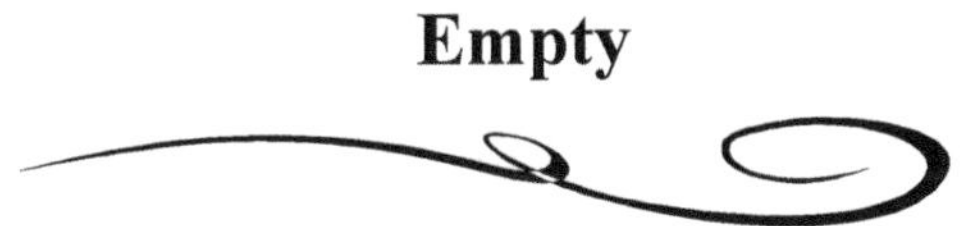

Barren like a willow tree when the winter's winds blows; empty like a rose garden after the freezing snow. Grounded like a butterfly with a broken wing, Silent like a little bird that cannot sing. Let me testify; let the tears fill up in my eyes. Ask me and I will say it's because of you I still can stand here today.

This is my biggest setback, and I'm feeling like I'm all by myself. So I'm calling on my LORD Jesus, because he is the only one who can see me through.

I'm so tired of being mistreated and playing the fool. Jesus, will you please help me get past my yesterdays. Because with you by my side, I know I can't be defeated.

Lately I've been feeling so hollow like a fallen tree, and sometimes unable to catch my breath like a fish out of sea. My Lord, I'm feeling like I lost my will to drive on like

An empty gas tank past "E."

I never at once felt so all alone, without being lost. This cold world has thrown my heart away like a coin being tossed.

Yet my soul stills belongs to you. Not that I would ever want to take it away from you, and I

praise you each day for all I have because you have given me a lot, but I feel so empty because blessings and gifts I have, but my own true love I have not.

All Alone

O' God hear me because I'm calling you; I'm sorry because I really don't know what I should do, because I can't stand this being all alone.

I find it easy to pray when my time feels far spent, or when my pockets are getting low and don't think I can pay my bills or the monthly rent. But these next words sometimes I find them hard to pray. But hear me when I say, that I can't stand it being here all alone.

Every day I wake up to give thanks for your grace and I'm living my life just to see your smiling face. But my God, deep in my heart of hearts there is still an empty space.

Because there are days when I stand and I sit, but then I try to over sleep, I can fast for days, then at times I will over eat. Lord this pain in my heart is something I just can't shake.

So that's why I'm writing you this letter to fight back the flow of tears. And though I'm praying to you without words or breath, I know every word you'll hear; because I said it before, but lately I can't stand it being here all alone.

Now as I write this letter I can feel your presents near, as a song I never heard before so softly plays in my ears. But forgive me Lord because I still feel that I need something just a little bit more.

Though if I fly on the wings of morning you would be the wind that lets me sore and if I sail the deepest sea you would be there to guide me, so I wouldn't have to roam.

Even if I make my bed in hell I know you would be there beside me or pick me up and take me home. So Lord, to end my silent prayer, this is why I'm writing to you; because I believe there is nothing that you can't do. And in your word you said it's not good for man to be...

Alone.

April 1

On April 1st I had a dream that started off with her saying the word "yes". Then I wrapped my arms around her; closed my eyes and I slowly pulled her close to my chest.

No dream has ever felt this way before, so I took a chance and gently began to press, her lips to mine.

Then I slowly exhaled and longed to hear the word again "yes" because no woman has ever been this real to me before. Could it be she stepped out of my dreams just to knock at my door?

I would give her the key if she just promised to never leave; and tell me her search is for love and not to play tricks or to deceive me.

This may be the only dream that I have to wake up to see or adore. I'm telling you now, my search is for love, so if you just take my hand together we can walk this long road and explore.

Could You be Her?

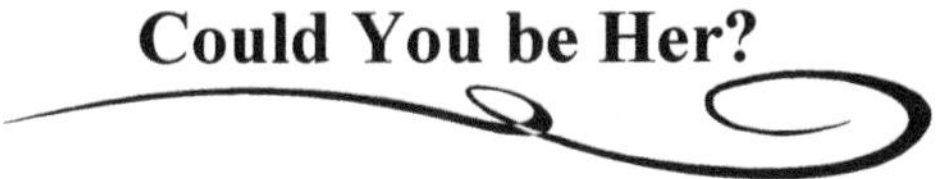

Only time will truly let us know if we will hold on tight or let this thing go, even though late nights I have to fight myself just to hit the door. Because as I look into your eyes, just one question keeps racing through my mind; tell me, could you be her?

She has touched me in a way that I won't soon forget, along with angel soft kisses on my neck. So while I can, I'll hold her close and kiss her just because she's mine.

But deep inside my heart I can't help from asking myself; could it be her?

Sometimes I day dream of her and me, arm in arm, slow dancing or just laying together reading each other poetry.

The two of us seem to go together like a fish in sea, some nights I would call just to hear her breathe.

"Dear, Lord please tell me, could it be her?"

Girl I got to let you know, you got your hooks in me, the way you keep me up late night on the phone while we're losing sleep.

Your style and grace blows my mind too, that's why I want just to be with you.

But only time will truly let us know if we should hold on tight or let this thing go, even thought the same thought keep racing throw my mind, could you be her?

So Simple

Could it be that love is really so simple, but it's our lack of trust and faith that makes it so hard? You see I've learned there is a difference between love and war, true love shouldn't leave you with any scars. As I reminisced back over my days, I slowly began to see love shouldn't make you feel like a bird in a cage, instead love is more like a master key that sets you free.

Lately I have felt like a prisoner of war trapped in a cage without the master key. So I search for love, but the right woman hasn't come to me. Even though some good women has passed my way, it always seem like they can't stay.

Lord please answer me, why is it every time I hold a woman close I get a feeling that lets me know, she isn't for me.

Why?

Because she doesn't hold the master key;

And there are times when I would kneel and pray just to hear a small voice softly say, "She's not for you".

No? "So you got to let her go".

Over time I have learned that knowing the right thing to do but doing the wrong is a sin. Though letting go sometimes give me the blues, if I keep on holding on to this day dream of mine we will both lose.

Can somebody really help me by telling me, that love is really all so simple? Because my life is a war and I feel like I'm trapped in a cage, just waiting on the master key.

Waiting for love

Oh No

Oh no, no no, this one will not get away from me. No no, oh no. This isn't goodbye; we can shock the world, just wait and see.

Oh no, no, no! I refuse to write another poem of how I loved and lost, I refuse to take this loss I'm going to pay the cost. This won't be just another tale from my trips all around the world. I refuse to let this just be a story about another girl. I remember her two dark brown eyes deep enough to get lost at sea. Don't tell me to say goodbye because it's been years since I wanted anyone this close to me.

Even though mountains, oceans, and rivers stand between us, through the spirit we will stay in tune. Tell me have you seen her; she has a smile bright like the sun, and eyes that shimmer like the stars and moon? She came in my life so quickly like the holidays, and just like a holiday she left too soon.

So no, no no, this is not the end; oh no, she won't get away from me. I don't want to let her go but do I have a choice? Because if my Lord says no I will obey his voice; but if he says yes, we can shock the world.

And there be no more sad songs of how I miss my favorite girl.

We don't need another story of a long kiss goodbye.

We don't need another tale about sleepless nights.

So no no, oh no, don't go, just please stay with me, because I won't say goodbye.

She's Gone Again

It was all like a sweet dream or an early morning daze, because she came and went from my life like a mirage from a heat stroke summer's haze.

Isn't it funny how no matter how hard we try to hold on to time, it still seems to fly away? Because right about now she's on a one way plane to California and I'm already missing her face, because no else can fill her space.

Even though this was no sweet dream, it was much too clear to be a daze,

She's was too real to be a moorage because whenever I reached out to touch her she would never fade away.

This still doesn't change the fact that she's still somewhere far away and I can't see her face, Except for in my visions when I pray.

She was my holiday love and I would watch over her like an eager gardener waiting for a flower to bloom, she was my holiday love because like a holiday she came so quickly

And like a holiday

She left too soon.

Guilty Pens Have no Rhythm

Because you lied, I had to say goodbye and let go of all the years we shared.

I was so mad I couldn't even cry, so I never asked you why you lied;

I just silently let go of my best friend,

Even though what I felt may have been wrong,

I could have written you a thousand songs,

But now all I feel is guilt when I hold a pen.

So I'm never going to write the same, because love poems only have life when you've lived them.

And I will never write another poem with a pen, because guilty pens have no rhythm. I can never write a love song again, the way I wrote about you.

With great regret I take back all the love I gave,

And you can have back every lie and dirty game you played.

This old heart will never be the same because you made me feel things I that will refuse to say.

In my mind I thought you were meant to stay around but in reality for years you've been slowly floating away like the clouds.

And I will never write another poem with a pen, because guilty pens have no rhythm. I can never write a love song again, the way I wrote about you.

Love poems only have life when we've lived them.

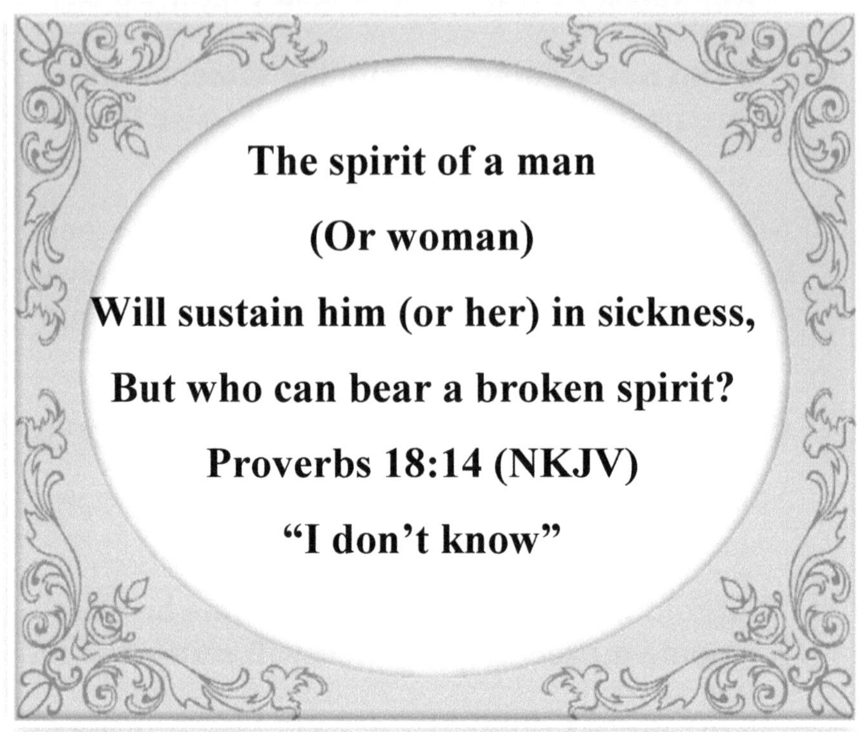
The spirit of a man
(Or woman)
Will sustain him (or her) in sickness,
But who can bear a broken spirit?
Proverbs 18:14 (NKJV)
"I don't know"

Letting Go Means Saying Good-Bye

These are three situations about a young man that had to come to an end and let a woman go. Some started off just so right, then they just began to fight and he had to let her go. One woman could see the real man within, but she had a husband and he couldn't stay in sin.

The last was his holiday love; she fit him like a glove but one day she had to leave.

Situation one,

He met her one dark night in a club, then on Christmas day she became the young man's love and he thought his life of loneliness had come to an end. But something just wasn't right, they lost their trust so they began to fuss and fight; now he's feeling like he's had more than enough. He swore he never wanted to see her again, the two them couldn't even be friends once they said goodbye. Because if she loved him, like she said did, then why would she lie?

Situation two,

They started off as just friends, even though she had a man, she kept trying to pull the young man closer. She was just a lonely heart and he needed love, but all they had was lust.

She would always push closer and he would pull away, then one day the young man tried to stay and she drug him down so low. Then he asks himself "if she cares about me, then why is she married?"

Humm… All the two of them had was sin; because she would cheat on the young man too if she would do it to him. So because she had a husband,

The young man needed to let her go.

Situation number three,

The young man knows the Lord's will must be but whatever it is he doesn't know.

He watched her pass him by so many times, and her face stays on his mind; although she doesn't know how he feels.

Their like passions made them friends, sharing their life's stories with just paper and a pen but they weren't meant to be.

She became the young man's holiday love, better than any other women mentioned just above, but his holiday moved away.

He helped her pack when it was time to go, to a place he didn't know, just that it was far from him.

If only the young man didn't have so much pride inside, maybe he could have knelt and cried because letting go sometimes means saying good-bye.

Each situation is about me, It's not the way I wanted it to be, but that's the way life goes.

Sometime relationships must come to an end, where we are unable to be friends, and you must turn your seared ways and let the relationships go.

The Masquerade

One day we should take the time to look over our lives and ask ourselves; am I really happy here or are my latent fears and guilty pleasures hindering my ways? As I took an objective look at the way I was living. It seems that I was dancing to the same song for years, while being lost among a number of costumed pretenders as if I was in a masquerade ball.

From the outside looking in at first you only see everyone moving and swaying as if they were one piece to a somber, yet sweet melody across a ballroom floor. All day and through the night, in sync we would stay, like the rolling waves of the ocean we rises and fall.

Is this really what you would call a celebration? I have been dancing for so long, my feet hurt. I also hate this song and I'm living a lie. A masquerade ball is a party though a charade, because no one is who they seem to be. With fake trust, false names, white gloves and porcelain masks to cover their faces. Can you see us in your mind now? Hand in hand with each other, though never really touching, due to the snow-white gloves we all wear. As we would glide almost hovering over the ballroom floor to a nonstop symphony of live instruments playing its hypnotic melody. If you close your eyes, then pause for a moment, you can hear the melody playing as each note is carried by the wind.

Are we really happy here? And though we hide behind porcelain white masks with a painted smile, no one knows what expression is truly on my face; then again they may not even care. So I have to ask myself, what is it that I'm afraid of? Why won't I allow the world see the real me? Could it be that what I really fear is

Removing my disguise and removing my security? Would my friends and family still love me? Would they still respect me, would they still be there for me, if one day I decided to be a drop of rain instead of a part of the bitter sea? Whenever I change does that mean I stop being me? No, it just means I stop being who you thought I was.

So I lose my grip of my dance partner hands, stand still in the mist of the crowd, without saying a word my silent resistance cries out loud. I strip away my disguises that have held me captive like belts and chains. Because I'm longing to feel and to be touched, I remove the white gloves then throw my hands in the air. I grab my mask with both hands and cast it down to watch it shatter on the floor, then I lift my head to the sky and leave my past behind, I put my defeat and hurt under my feet. And without a word or a wave of goodbye I walk

away before every painted porcelain eye of the Masquerade.

And I'm not looking back, though as I leave, lightly under that old somber yet sweet melody, a new symphony begins as the random sounds of porcelain mask falling across the ballroom floor fills the air, followed by foot steps behind me.

Are you truly happy this year, or are words and people getting in your way?

How long will you be a part of the worlds masquerade?

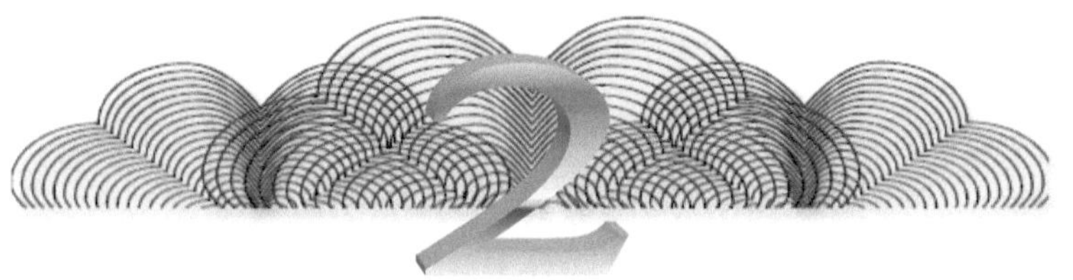

CHAPTER

After the Masquerade....

We Must Deal with The Mess We Made.

WEC

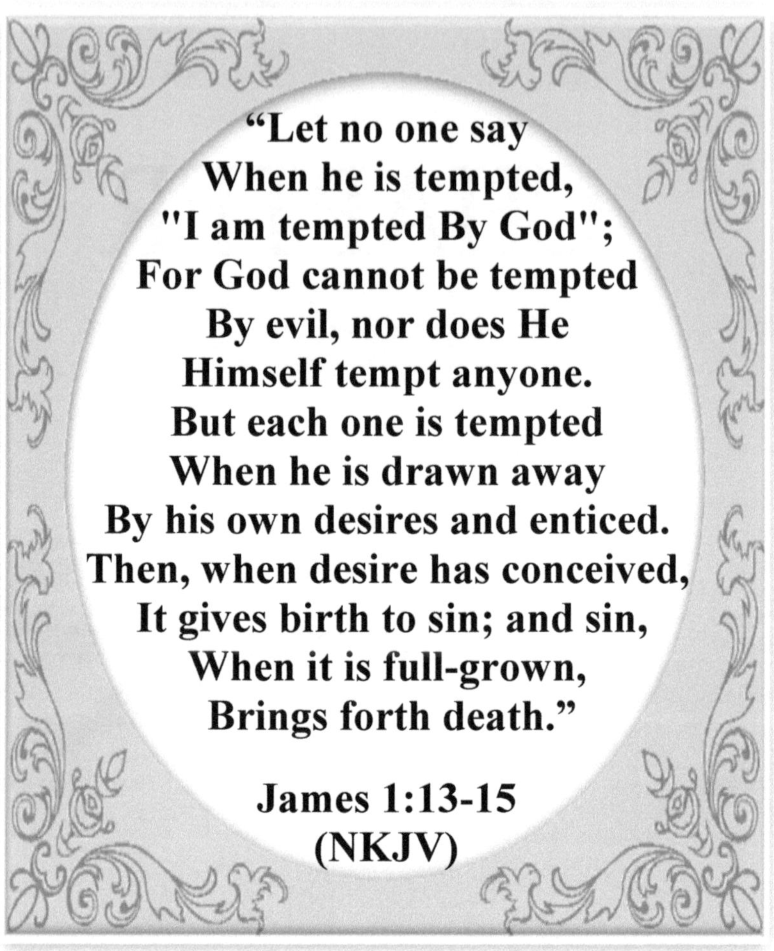

"I learn the hard way the reason why God tells us not to do certain things. It's not because He doesn't want us to have fun; it's because He doesn't want us to get hurt."

Now that we're done

Now that we're done what are you thinking? Now that we've gone too far, I can't stop from thinking, about the time we went there, without even thinking. And will we do it again? As we lay on a bed of broken trust, I can't stop wondering why I wasn't strong enough and was it really love or lust, because I don't know.

I didn't come to play any games, but if we just made love, then why do I feel so ashamed? The sensations from you lifted me on a natural high. But as my high comes down I really need to know.

Now that we're done, what are you thinking? Now that we've gone too far, I can't stop from thinking, because now we went there, without even thinking. And is this the end?

Awaking to the aftermath of sins pleasure is full of nothing but emptiness and pain; it's like a cloudless picnic suddenly overtaken by the rain.

The last night when we were together, it was real what I felt when I looked deep in your eyes. You only asked me one question, and I answered you with all of my might, but I sincerely wish I had also told you; that I couldn't spend the night.

Because now it's six in the morning and the sun is starting to rise, as we lay face to face. I have to look you in your eyes to ask you these next questions, because there's nothing left to hide. And what I feel in my heart is something I just can't deny.

So tell me, now that we're done what are you thinking? Now that we've gone too far, I can't stop from thinking, about last night when we went there, without even thinking? And will we do it again? Or will this be the end?

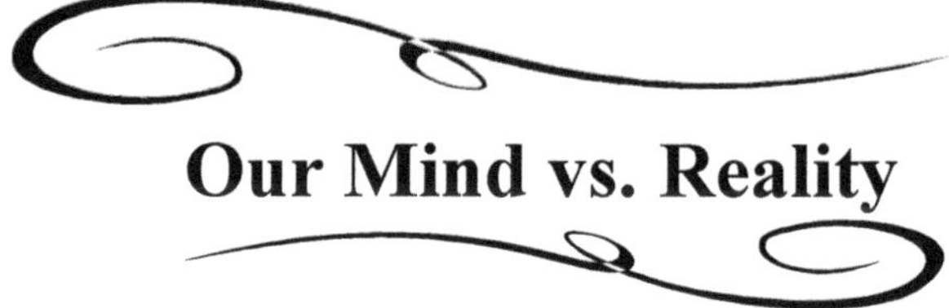

Our Mind vs. Reality

In our minds we will always be more than friends, but in reality we can never be the same.

In reality we haven't danced in years, but in my mind we will never dance our last dance.

In my mind we have made love a thousand times, but in reality we have never even kissed.

In reality our friendship came to an end, but in my mind I always thought I would see you again.

In our minds we always hoped we would last, but in reality our dreams faded away with the past.

In reality our relationship is soon to be doomed, but in our minds our hearts remain in tuned.

In our minds we only see what we want life to be, but in reality we are really searching blindly.

In my mind I run to put my problems and hurts behind me, but in reality I'm just trying to run away.

Cold World

It seems so many people are running a race through life, that would be sudden death if they ever stop, but no matter how far they run, they will never run off the edge of this cold,

Cold world.

I seen so many people trying to reach heaven on clouds of smoke, but it's at cloud nine where they always stop, but as soon as the high fades away they all quickly fall back down to this cold,

Cold world.

I would take long trips in wine carriages searching for peace on every green hill and mountaintop. But once the bottles ran dry, I found myself lost in this cold,

Cold world.

**So many people will set their sails to sea taking their feet off of the solid Rock. But when the water gets troubled they find out even at the bottom of ocean it's still a cold,
Cold world.**

"And God spake all these words, saying, I am the LORD thy God, which have brought thee out of the land of Egypt, out of the house of bondage. Thou shalt have no other gods before me."

Exodus 20:1-3: (KJV)

I Remember Egypt

I remember Egypt. Egypt was once home to me, and like a person very closes to me.

I remember Egypt. Egypt gave me everything I wanted though never what I needed. She would ignore my feelings but feed my greed.

I remember Egypt, Egypt was once my old lover and a provider. With the same lips she made me Love her, she also caused me to despise her.

I remember Egypt. Egypt was a place where I could drink till I fell asleep, yet never find rest. I would lay my head on her warm bosom every night but never heard a heart beat in her chest.

I remember Egypt. Egypt was my strong hold a dark prison covered with fear. She was like a head with only a mouth and no place to hear.

I remember Egypt. Because of my gifts and beauty, Egypt loved to be seen with me in public places, though when I received more attention than her, she quickly revealed other faces.

I remember Egypt, Egypt spoke no truths and filled my heart with lies; she knows no love and would not weep if I died.

Egypt was the place of my bondage and the sources of my weakness; she was my Delilah, my thorn and pain. Egypt was the old love I gladly left in Jesus' name.

I remember Egypt

*"If we want to become a part of the world's solutions in our life time,
We first must stop being a part of its problems."*

Clean out your Closet

Let the past be just that, the past, let it go and never pick it back up. It's time to go deeper and look into the forgotten places; tonight it's time to clean out your closet.

Fights not won, letters never returned, and calls not answered. Hurts, pains, grudges, and broken dreams, none of them are what they seem.

The past didn't make you who you are, God did.

So there's no reason to hold on and store those tarnished memories inside you.

Open the door to your heart and clean out your closet.

Give the keys to God and he will remove all things that you don't need, the painful past can't help you, so if you're ready and willing to submit. Peace will be yours, but first you must to clean out your closet.

In Jesus name

Mirror, Mirror on the Wall

Mirror, mirror on the wall, I don't care if you should ever fall, because there is no such thing as bad luck. Twinkle, twinkle little star up above the world so very far, there will be no more wishes for you at night because you can never hear or see me.

And to all the coins in the wishing wells that were kissed to be sealed with a wish that they would never tell, I pray your coins rust and the water runs dry because through you wishes can never be.

Mirror, mirror on the wall, with both hands I will knock you off my wall, because my future is something you can never see. Twinkle, twinkle little star, you can burn out right where you are, because your light will never ease my pain.

And as I walk down the street splitting poles and letting every black cat cross my path, I will look to only one book for soul searching because the zodiac is trash. So while the midnight rain covers the falling stars and refills the wishing wells, and as the glowing rainbow parts the skies, just know that the real treasure at the end is a promise from God not a pot of gold that should lie.

Jesus You are my guiding light when I'm lost, and You are my hope when the world believes there is none. To my best friend

Thank you Jesus Christ

A HERO

My Lord, there have been days I've been so sick and tired of my life; I never thought a change would come, no, never.

Wishing on falling stars or dropping pennies into wishing wells, saying whatever.
I was looking for a hero to call on, or a dream to hold on to, wanting the things of this world.

But if a super hero could save me, I wouldn't know You today. And if the stars could hear me; I would have sprouted wings and flown away. And if the whole world were mine to hold on to, then I could never be saved.

Jesus is the only hero we should call on through the good and bad times of our days. He would still know your heart, if the stars never fell, there were no coins in the wishing wells, or if all our dreams began to fade away.

To my Hero, *Thank you Jesus Christ*

Jesus said:

"Come to me, all you who are weary

And burdened, and I will give you rest.

Take my yoke upon you and learn from me,

For I am gentle and humble in heart,

And you will find rest for your souls.

For my yoke is easy and my burden is light."

Matthew 11:28-30 (NIV)

A Psalm for 2006

It would be foolish of me to think that I could ever successfully tell a lie to someone like You, a friend closer than a brother like You. It's just that whenever Your Holy Spirit is around I feel like a baby eagle who is ready to spread his wings and sore but needs his father to teach him much more. I often wonder could it be Yourself that You see inside of me that keeps You waiting for me.

So, Oh God, my God please teach and use all of me.

I call you Jesus, my God, my Fire, my hero, my Rain, and even my Heart's Burning Flame because whenever I needed You the most You were right there. But why is it sometimes when I preach before crowds, pray or lay my hands, I can't always feel You there? Father I'm still that same baby eagle learning to sore, I'm still willing to let your Holy Spirit fill my wings and teach me more. Could it be their unbelief that You see, or is it something inside of me?

So, Oh, God, my God please don't let fear make a liar or a fool out of me.

I gave up my old life and left some friends even my family doesn't fully understand how

I've change and all that I left for only You. I left the life and world I adored, when You called me by name and promised me much more. You are The Most High God who has given me everything that I need, though there is more that I want from You and I know there is so much more that You will require of me.

So, Oh God, my God, please keep teaching and using all of me. And Oh, God, my God, please don't let fear make a liar or a fool out of me.

Candlestick

You are my candlestick, burning in
the night. So I may see,

Just a single flame and You light my
way.

You're just a simple light to show my
path.

So small You are, but You burn so
bright with the softest light.

And You burn for just me.

Everywhere else is darkness, so from
my candle I will not stray.

You are my eternal guide, and Your
light will never fade away.

Thank you Father for your Holy
Spirit

Amen

The Blues

As I give my life to Jesus, slowly my past pains begins to ease away; although sometimes I fall on my face after praying on my knees at the end of the day. I wonder if anyone will ever know, I wrote so many songs and a few poems or two, all about my life of love but mostly about my life of the blues. Lord I'm just a child in love with the twilight after the sunset… stormy skies, poetry and the blues.

As each year fades away, I stare into the southern moon, because making wishes on falling stars never comforts me when I'm feeling down, but still I stay up to see them anyhow.

So when I'm all alone and no one knows or cares, Yahweh plays a symphony to remedy me, with His Holy Spirit in the air. Then I put my feeling to paper as his song stirs my mood. A feeling like the colors of the many waters, called the blues.

Thinking back in my mind I can only remember three golden sunsets and one glowing sunrise, but I recall a million gray stormy skies and a thousand soft evening twilights. I remember the first time the cold wind blew and a snowflake touched my face; my very first kiss and the memory my first sweet love, can never be replaced. But now, Father my heart is Your

House and Your home though the blues still lives here too. So next time You're on Your way home, can You bring just a little more love, and play a song so I can write about my life of blues

There are days when I still find by myself looking for Your face in the misty rain and morning dew. Sometimes on the beach in the salt-water waves, though they're always black and brown; but most often, I'm looking to the endless skies, because just like I feel they are blue.

"One of the hardest

Thing I ever did in life was

To learn how to wait.

But I learned when you're waiting

For the right Thing for the right

Reason it's always worth it."

"Hope deferred (delayed)
It makes the heart sick, But
When the desire comes,
It is a tree of life."

Proverbs 13:12
(NKJV)

The Fools Game

A songwriter writes a question,

"What is Love?"

But never expects an answer. As he sits and slowly ponder on how people go through brake- up's to make-up's, looking left to right and all around the world, when what they really need sits on high above the ribbons in the skies and just beyond the light of the southern moon.

How high?

Up there clouds cease to form as water freezes,

The mighty eagle can't fly and the light that shines can't be looked upon by the human eyes.

Again the writer thinks to himself and writes, "It seems like everybody wants somebody but, nobody want the person that wants them."

Hmm.., why is this?

Just another question without good an answer.

He comes to this conclusion; to fall in love is to play *The Fools game.*

It's easy to play the fools game, when two people don't feel the same.

When do we play the fools game? When a man and woman's love start to gradually change.

How many of us have played the fools game?

When we held on through heartaches, bad time, war and even freezing rain;

It's so easy to play this fools game, when you lay down your life for people who may never change.

When was the last time you played the fools game?

I'm playing right here right now, sitting in this city alone waiting for someone to come home and change.

How long will I play the fools game?

The truth is, I'll keep playing until my time runs out, my love change, or until she starts to feels the same.

Am I a fool in love or just in love with being a fool, patently holding a royal hand in this game?

Lastly, the writer makes a closing thought; who is the real fool?

Is it the one who waits on love, or the one who throws in the towel before the end of the game?

Because anything worth having is worth working for; anything worth working for is worth fighting for. Anything worth fighting for is worth waiting for.

Now who wants to play the fools game?

The End of a Chase

Some may call me a fool, but I can't help it. It was my choice to hold on while you kept passing by me.

But I don't have to chase you anymore, I'm the one you adore; I never thought falling in love would go this smooth.

As I think back I can't remember ever feeling this way about anybody. Even when I tried to move on my heart would find its way back to you.

But I don't have to chase you anymore, because I'm the one you adore, I never thought love would come this soon.

This must be GOD, because I never would have planned my own life out like this, I never thought I could fall in love with a woman whom I've never kissed.

I know before we see each other it's going to be awhile. I know before we can be together it's going to be awhile so I'm praying and praying that our love will grow and stay in GOD.

After chasing you for so long my heart had grown sore but I don't have to anymore because I'm the one you adore.

And you came to me before it was too late for love.

You called to say GOD had opened your eyes and you could now see.

You called to say you have fallen in love with me.

You called just to say you wanted to have a family.

You called to say it was our destiny.

You called just to say it wasn't too late for true and pure love.

"Lord,

Make me to know my end,

And what is the measure of my days,

That I may know how frail I am.

Indeed, you have made my days as

Handbreadths,

And my age is as nothing before you;

Certainly every man at his best state

Is but vapor.

Selah"

Psalms 39:4-5 (NKJV)

Who am I?

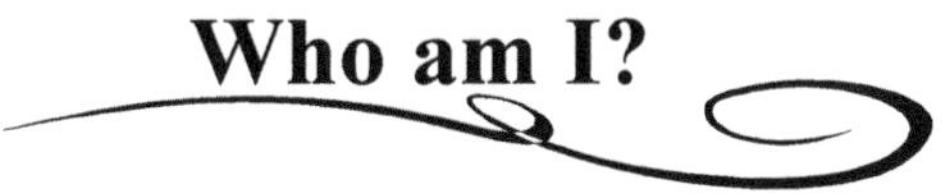

After over 26 years I believe I finally know the meaning of life

And all the purposes I have been put here for.

Because as a child I thought I was born just to be my father's son.

As teenager I thought I would spend the rest of my life as a fool.

Later, as a young man felt I was called to be in the army, but in my heart it just didn't seem right.

Then at the age of 22 I gave my life to Jesus Christ and I didn't fully understand who I was because my heart and life hadn't change right away

Until the glory of God shined through all the gray and His light showed me the way.

Today I know who I am and I know why I'm here. Even though I don't always know where I'm going, I know where I am.

But who am I?

To my family I'm still a son and a brother.

Who am I?

I am a simple man, a child of the Most High God and a prophet.

Who am I?

I am a friend to some and one day a husband and a father.

Who am I?

I'm much more than just a color.

I am

Willman Edward Compton Jr. III

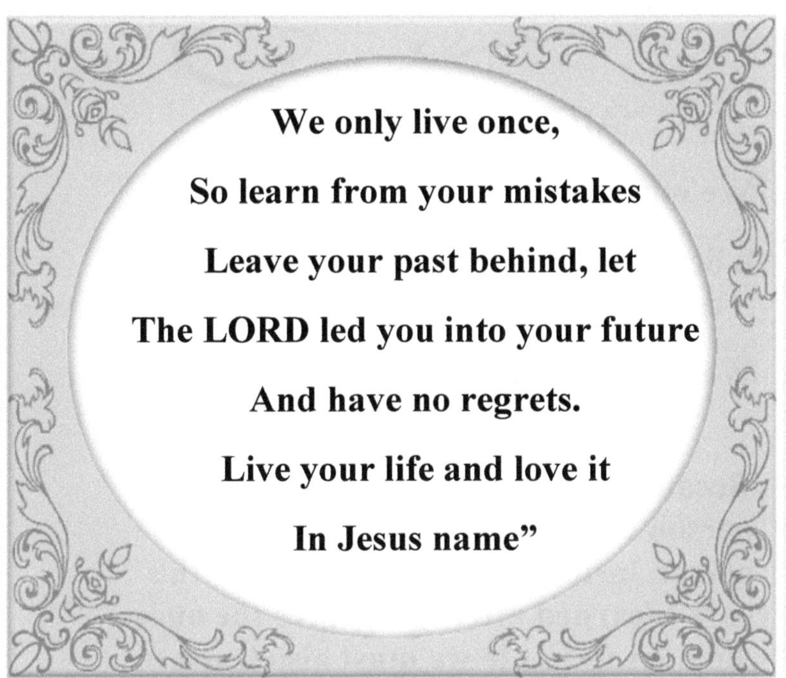

Willman E, Compton Jr III

“After the Masquerade

We must deal with the mess we made,

All lies start to fade but the hurt that was caused seems to still hang around.

We must step out of the day dreams in our minds to face reality

Because only then will we see that the person causing us the most hurt is the person inside of you and me. Over the years I learned after we forgive the ones who hurt us in life we must also learn to forgive ourselves.”

The book After the Masquerade is a collection of poems about me realizing my mistakes trying to learn from them, and moving on with my life.

Not always an easy thing to do… But it’s something that must be done.”

Thanks and Blessings

To My father and God in Heaven who inspired me and gave me the gift to write my life's story thank you. To my big sister and little brother in Christ Kindra Benson, James Watts , Alynthia Washington, the Arms family Ron &Tina. To My family the Compton's /Hamilton's/ Fannin's, my mother, my father, Lonnie, Chella, Tammy, Terrell, Chaz, and Jazz I love you all and thanks for supporting and believing in me . To my Pastor Rob and First Lady Tresa, as well as my entire E.C.C church family, I thank you for all you have done and are doing for me in my life.

May God bless all the works of your hands

In Jesus Christ's name

WORKS CITED

Bible Verses:

Exodus 20:1-3: (KJV)

Psalms 39:4-5 (NKJV)

Proverbs 5:1-6 (NKJV)

Proverbs 13:12 (NKJV)

Proverbs 18:14 (NKJV)

Matthew 7:4-5(NKJV)

Matthew 11:28-30 (NIV)

James 1:13-1 5 (NKJV)

Philippians 3:13-14 *(*NKJV*)*

Webster's online Dictionary

http://www.merriam-webster.com/dictionary.htm

The Definitions of Masquerade (\□mas-kə-□rād\)

Song

"No Woman no Cry" by Bob Marley

All other quotes by:

Willman E. Compton Jr. III

Also From Rain Maker's Publishing Inc.

30 DAYS OF JESUS CHRIST A BIBLE STUDY TOOL
BY
WILLMAN E. COMPTON JR

International Standard Book Number: 978-0-557-42125-1

Cover Design & Book Layout: Willman Compton Jr

Contact Author: WILLMANCOMPTON@ATT.NET

PAIN FOR A PURPOSE

By Becky E. Davis

To contact Author: beckydavis35@yahoo.com

Printed in USA

Rain Maker's Publishing

Thank You

For allowing me to share a small part of my life with you,

There will be more to come…

www.ingramcontent.com/pod-product-compliance
Ingram Content Group UK Ltd.
Pitfield, Milton Keynes, MK11 3LW, UK
UKHW041914190726
13854UKWH00003B/1240

9 780557 432653